BASIC ✳ ESSENTIALS™
COOKING IN THE OUTDOORS

Help Us Keep This Guide Up to Date

Every effort has been made by the author and editors to make this guide as accurate and useful as possible. However, many things can change after a guide is published—new products and information become available, regulations change, techniques evolve, etc.

We would love to hear from you concerning your experience with this guide and how you feel it could be improved and be kept up to date. While we may not be able to respond to all comments and suggestions, we'll take them to heart and we'll also make certain to share them with the author. Please send your comments and suggestions to the following address:

The Globe Pequot Press
Reader Response/Editorial Department
P.O. Box 833
Old Saybrook, CT 06475

Or you may e-mail us at:

editorial@globe-pequot.com

Thanks for your input, and happy travels!

BASIC ESSENTIALS™ SERIES

BASIC ✳ ESSENTIALS™
COOKING IN THE
OUTDOORS

SECOND EDITION

CLIFF JACOBSON

ILLUSTRATIONS BY CLIFF MOEN

The Globe Pequot Press

Old Saybrook, Connecticut

Cover design by Lana Mullen
Illustrations on pages 16, 21, 31, 34 by Diane Blasius;
    all others by Cliff Moen.
Text and layout design by Casey Shain

Basic Essentials is a trademark of The Globe Pequot Press.

Library of Congress Cataloging-in-Publication Data
Jacobson, Cliff.
        Basic essentials: cooking in the outdoors/by
    Cliff Jacobson; illustrations by Cliff Moen.—(2nd ed.)
            p. c.m. — (Basic essentials series)
        Includes index.
    ISBN 0-7627-0426-8
        1. Outdoor cookery. I. Title. II. Series.
    TX823.J33   1999
    641.5'78—DC21   98-49454
                                                      CIP

♻ Printed on recycled paper
Printed and bound in Quebec, Canada
Second Edition/First Printing

Dedication

In memory of my loving wife, Sharon Jacobson, whose life was cut short by an asthma attack.

Contents

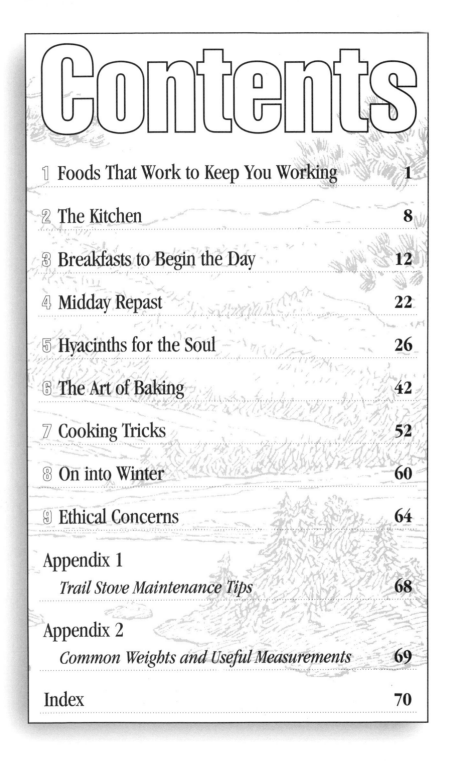

Preface

Dear Reader,

I really thought I had my act together in 1989, when I wrote *Basic Essentials: Cooking in the Outdoors*. I've learned a lot since then, and you'll find lots of new stuff in this updated edition.

New foods and recipes come and go; there's always something new to try. But what hasn't changed are the skills you need to prepare great meals when the weather turns sour. For example: how do you make spaghetti for six on a hot, one-burner trail stove without burning and gluing the pasta to the pot bottom? How do you preserve fresh vegetables so they'll last two weeks on a camping trip? Can you make pizza without an oven and cook fish without a pan? Does a *good* lightweight frying pan really exist? Is it possible to prepare classy meals for six—and keep them hot long enough for everyone to enjoy seconds— when it's pouring ice-cold rain and blowing bloody murder?

You'll find the answers to these questions and more in this new edition of *Basic Essentials: Cooking in the Outdoors*. You'll also find some great new recipes, but the real emphasis of this book is on *meal management skills*. If recipes are what you want, buy a cookbook! Any "indoor meal" can be prepared outdoors if you substitute camping-compatible dried products for fresh ones and master the meal management tricks contained in this book.

—*Cliff Jacobson*

Foods That Work to Keep You Working

Whenever I return from one of my lengthy canoe trips in the Canadian wilds, someone invariably broaches the subject of foods. What kind and how much do I bring? How do I pack crushables such as eggs, crackers, and breads so they won't be mashed inside heavy packsacks? Are there inexpensive plastic containers that won't leak after a month on the trail? On a long trip, fresh foods are out. And except for special occasions, so are cans. How then, do I accommodate variety and good taste? A steady diet of oatmeal, peanut butter, and Hamburger Helper may be nutritious enough, but it doesn't inspire excitement.

Then there's the not-so-simple matter of preparing foods in the field. Whipping up a gourmet meal in a major downpour calls for procedural skills that you won't find in cookbooks.

In the heat of discussion, someone always brings up the subject of nutrition. That a food tastes good, looks appetizing, and provides plenty of energy for a strenuous outing isn't good enough. This individual wants to know how the nutritional value of each entree compares with U.S. Recommended Daily Allowances.

That a balanced diet is as important in the woods as at home is a forgone fact. But how scientific do you have to be when planning an outdoor cuisine? Not very—as long as you apply common sense and don't rely too much on a few good things. What works at home will work in the wilds—with one exception: calories! You need lots of 'em— 4,000 or more per day if you're really working hard. By comparison, a typical homemaker expends about 1,400 calories a day, an office worker about 2,500, and a factory worker approximately 3,000 calories.

An average hunter, hiker, or canoeist will burn about five calories per minute (300 per hour, 2,400 per eight-hour day); a cross-country skier, biker, mountaineer, or backpacker may use twice that amount. Keep in mind the obvious fact that extra work requires extra fuel. If you provide an assortment of foods from which to choose, you'll have no problems with nutritional components or complaints. However, if you must pursue a scientific course, just remember that a pound of body fat contains about 3,500 calories. With this knowledge, plus a calorie/nutrition chart (available in every food's text), you can easily plan meals that will retain your body weight and keep everyone happy.

Fortunately, you don't need to be too scientific in determining nutritional value because your body's natural craving for variety will help you make sound food choices. Simply know to which food group each edible belongs (fats, carbohydrates, proteins), and "weigh" your daily food intake so it corresponds roughly to the following formula.

Carbohydrates

Carbohydrates provide quick energy and should supply at least 50 percent of your daily requirement—easy enough as these are everyone's favorite food group. Breads, cereals, honey (honey and tea is the traditional north country drink), jam, dehydrated fruits, cookies, and candy are rich in carbohydrates.

Fat

Fats contain more than twice as many calories per pound as carbohydrates and are the body's major source of stored energy. They also carry the fat-soluble vitamins—A, D, E, and K. Generally speaking, fats should provide about one-fifth of your daily intake of calories, though for a really tough trip that amount should be increased substantially. Except in calorie-burning winter, when you might go as high as 40 percent, 25 percent is a good ballpark figure. (You need more oxygen to metabolize fats than carbohydrates or proteins. For this reason, fat intake should be reduced when working at high altitudes [above 12,000 feet]).

Admittedly, it's hard to carry a lot of high-fat foods on a backcountry trip without significantly increasing pack weight and bulk. Examples of foods that contain fats are margarine (I prefer Parkay liquid), cooking oil, nuts and peanut butter, cheese, bacon, and sausage.

Because fats aren't converted to energy as fast as the other food groups, they allow us to go without eating for long periods of time. Verlen Kruger, who amazed the world by paddling his solo canoe

28,000 miles in three years, once commented that his favorite food was pancakes, smothered with margarine (a primary fat source). Verlen said he could travel "five miles per pancake!"

Protein

The typical 160-pound adult needs about 45 grams (1.6 ounces) of useable protein per day. But for traveling the backcountry you'll need much more. A hearty breakfast of oat or wheat cereal and reconstituted dry milk; a lunch that includes cheese, beef jerky, peanut butter or sausage; and a supper that contains dehydrated or freeze-dried meat (or if you're really enterprising, fresh fish) will provide all the protein you need.

Note: **Proteins are not stored to any great extent in the body, so those eaten in excess of energy and tissue repair requirements will be converted to glycogen and stored as fat. For this reason, it's best to space protein intake throughout the day, rather than to ingest it at a single sitting. Moreover, if your calorie count is insufficient for the activity and there are no carbohydrates or fats available to supply energy, the proteins you eat will be converted directly to glucose (energy). For this reason, you're wise to combine some other high-energy food with your protein snack to get full nutrition from it.**

Vitamins and Minerals

It's only on extended (several months) trips that you need to be concerned about vitamins and minerals. Even then, don't worry, as a balanced diet invariably contains everything you need. Only the water-soluble vitamins (the B and C group) must be replenished regularly. And that's no problem if you supplement your meals with vitamin C-fortified fruit drinks, jams, and dehydrated fruits, and vitamin B-rich cereals.

Foods That Work

Freeze-dried and dehydrated foods. The best dried foods taste as good or better than canned fare but are lighter and more compact. If you stick with supermarket entrees, they are quite inexpensive.

Nonetheless, a few carefully selected canned goods (please carry out the cans!) are a welcome addition on most wilderness trips. The sage advice that "cans have no place on a wilderness trip" applies only to places where cans aren't allowed—such as the Boundary Waters Canoe Area of Minnesota—and to backpacking ventures where every ounce counts.

Freeze-dried foods. Fresh or cooked foods are flash frozen and placed in a vacuum, which draws off about 98 percent of the moisture by evaporating the ice at temperatures of -50° Fahrenheit or so. The freeze-dried food is then sealed in moisture, and oxygen-proof packaging. The food retains its original shape and texture and most of its good taste. Shelf life is measured in decades. Freeze-drying is frightfully expensive, however. For example, one ounce of freeze-dried hamburger or chicken costs more than a dollar!

Food Dehydration

Most foods dehydrate well. Exceptions are steaks, chops, chicken, fish, and shellfish, which are best freeze-dried or canned. Dehydration is slow and messy, and it requires lots of preparation time. Nonetheless, if you do a lot of lightweight camping, it's worth drying the three foods that form the basis of the most popular trail meals—ground beef, beans, and tomato sauce.

How to Dehydrate Ground Beef

Dehydrated hamburger is a major component of spaghetti, chili, stews, stroganoff, and enchiladas. I used to buy expensive freeze-dried ground beef until I discovered that dehydrated hamburger tastes as good. Ground beef should be as lean as possible.

PROCEDURE

1. Brown the meat and chop it into very tiny pieces as it cooks.

2. Spoon the browned hamburger into a strainer and allow the fat to drain. Then pour a full kettle of boiling water over the hamburger. The hot water will remove nearly all the fat (which can cause the meat to spoil) and leach some nutrients, but not flavor, from the meat.

3. Place several sheets of thick paper toweling on the dehydrator tray and spread out the well-drained hamburger on the toweling. One pound of hamburger per tray is about right. Set the dehydrator temperature to 140° Fahrenheit or "high." The meat will be dry and ready to package in twenty-four hours.

How to Dry Canned Beans

I use dried beans in chili, burritos, soups, and stews. Canned beans are easy to dry and they rehydrate in minutes.

Canned beans can be dried with or without the syrup. I prefer without.

PROCEDURE

1. Pour the canned beans into a strainer and allow most of the syrup to drain out.

2. Line the dehydrator tray with a Teflon sheet or plastic wrap, then pour the beans on top. Even out the beans to a one-bean-thick layer.

3. Turn the dehydrator to "high." The beans are dry when they're rock hard—about twelve hours.

How to Make Tomato Powder

Tomato powder—made from canned tomato sauce or paste or your favorite spaghetti sauce—can be used in any recipe that calls for fresh tomatoes, tomato paste, or sauce. One tablespoon of powder equals one medium tomato or about ½ cup of fresh puree. Dilute the powder to the thickness you need.

PROCEDURE

1. Line the dehydrator tray with plastic wrap and pour the sauce (canned or your own recipe) onto the wrap. Turn the heat to "high" and dry the sauce until it's leathery and the top is dry to the touch. Then turn the "leather" over and remove the plastic wrap. Allow the back side to dry until the leather is brittle—about eight hours.

2. Break the crisp tomato sheet into small pieces and powder the pieces in a *dry* blender or seed mill. Package the powder in an airtight container.

If this seems like too much work, order tomato powder from your local co-op. You'll discover the cost is shocking—nearly $20 a pound at this writing!

Vacuum-Seal Your Meals

During the summer I outfit and guide canoe trips in northern Canada for the Science Museum of Minnesota. The trips last one to three weeks. There's no refrigeration on a wilderness canoe trip, so I vacuum-seal my foods to prevent spoilage. Vacuum sealing also reduces bulk, which saves pack space. I rely on a Foodsaver by Tilia (800-777-5452) to vacuum-seal all my meals. My machine is twelve years old and it has never let me down. Vacuum sealing extends the life of all foods and makes meals waterproof. Here are some examples, based on my experience.

Approximate Shelf Life of Foods

Food	Double-Sealed in Ziploc Bags	Vacuum-Sealed
Fresh pita bread	2 weeks	4 weeks
Bagels (no preservatives)	3 days	1 week
Dehydrated hamburger	2 weeks	1 year
Dehydrated chili beans	3 weeks	1 year

I vacuum-seal everything that comes in flimsy or non-waterproof containers. Examples include candy bars, cereals, rice, and pasta. Long spaghetti becomes rigid, rock-hard, and virtually unbreakable (you could kill a bear with it!) when it's vacuum-sealed.

Tip: **If you don't own a vacuum sealing machine, double-seal your food in Ziploc bags. Insert a drinking straw in the corner of each bag and suck out the air as you seal the opening. A partial vacuum seal will result.**

As important as dried foods are to the success of a backcountry outing they alone don't supply enough energy to keep bodies humming happily. As mentioned, you need lots of calories on a tough trip, and that means extra amounts of breadstuffs, peanut butter, margarine, nuts, cereals, and cheese. All wilderness foods should be lightweight, slow to spoil, easy to prepare, and stable in hot weather. These requirements alone necessarily eliminate many otherwise excellent products from your shopping list.

You'll also want to know which foods *really* work to keep you working and which don't. And you won't find that information on a calorie chart or from nutritionists who don't camp. That's because a food can look good on paper and be completely worthless on the trail. A good example is Moose Juice.

Moose Juice was a product of the mind of Verlen Kruger and the 1966 Atikoken, Ontario, to Ely, Minnesota, canoe race. The Atikoken to Ely run was once touted as the toughest canoe race on the continent, and with good reason. Equipped with only the bare essentials of a canoe, map and compass, rain gear, and food, competitors would paddle nonstop to Ely, 55 miles away. After a rest they'd run back again at top speed. The 110-mile route included twenty-eight grueling portages, several huge lakes, and an occasional bog. Navigating in the dark called for a high degree of resourcefulness; most canoe teams never finished the race; many canoeists became lost. (Evidently the Ely to Atikoken race ultimately proved too tough as it has since been discontinued for lack of competitors.)

To supply his body with the energy necessary to maintain the quick sixty-stroke-per-minute cadence used in canoe racing, Verlen developed a "complete nutritional liquid supplement," which he affectionately named "Moose Juice." When Clint Waddell, Verlen's partner, learned of the nutrient concoction, he objected strongly. But Verlen, a soft-spoken man of infinite patience, pointed out that Moose Juice was a product of modern science. It met every nutritional requirement, didn't need to be unwrapped or cooked, and could be consumed on the run.

Clint wasn't convinced so he hid away a few sticks of beef jerky "just in case." Good thing, too: "Just in case" came about four hours into the race when Clint became violently ill from the effects of the home-made brew. The beef jerky helped some, but not enough. In the end, the Moose Juice won and Clint and Verlen lost the race.

That episode points out an obvious but often ignored food fact: *The physical makeup of foods must not be so unusual that they disagree with your system!* And since one person's system rejects what another's relishes, you'd best stay away from fancy or unusual edibles until you've first tried them under fire—that is, the fire of your own kitchen stove.

You may also find that your body dislikes "sameness" in foods. A continuous diet of oatmeal, dried milk, dehydrated fruit, and peanut butter may be scientifically acceptable fare, but your stomach may refuse it anyway. No need to prepare gourmet delights to please your system, but you may want to give it a few simple food options to choose from.

The old Northwest Company did a lot of research on foods during the fur-trade days of the seventeenth and eighteenth centuries. They found that pemmican was the only food that a man could tolerate for long periods of time. Seventeenth-century pemmican usually consisted of pressed buffalo meat with a generous amount of buffalo grease added. The voyageurs often mixed the pemmican with flour and water and cooked up a substantial soup called "rubbaboo," which they heartily devoured daily for weeks at a time. Even today, pemmican is considered an excellent trail food, though most wilderness travelers never learn to develop a taste for it.

Okay, enough about nutrition and food hokum. Time now to check out specific foods and the methods for preparing them.

The Kitchen

hen it comes to cooking in the outdoors, you can't do good work without good tools. Badly designed, flimsy cookware won't do. Unfortunately, most pots and pans you buy for camping are awful.

Note: **I receive no royalties for suggesting certain products, even ones I designed. In fact, many of the items I recommend in my books came about only after I badgered manufacturers to produce them to my own high standards. When I find something I really like, I want to share it with my friends.**

For a party of four, you'll need the following gear:

Three nesting pots with covers. Pots may be aluminum, stainless steel, or porcelain-lined carbon steel. I prefer stainless because it resists dents and is easy to clean. Where weight and bulk is a primary concern, the kit can be reduced to two pots. Some backpackers travel with only a single pot. Two-and-one-half cups of hot food is a reasonable serving size for a hungry camper. Your largest pot should have a sixteen-cup capacity so you can cook pasta without gluing it to the bottom.

Tip: **Engrave lines on the inside pot sides at one-cup intervals and write the total capacity (e.g. sixteen cups) just below the rim. This forethought will eliminate guesswork and the need for measuring cups at mealtime.**

For faster and more even heating, you may want to blacken aluminum pot bottoms. A few sessions over a campfire will do it and so will Alumablack—a chemical agent used for darkening aluminum gun parts. Similar to "cold blue," every gun shop has it.

One relatively straight-sided, 10- or 12-inch diameter, Teflon-lined skillet. You need one skillet for every five people. Or, you can bring a grill that spans two stoves. Skillets and grills should be Teflon (or similar substance) coated, carbon steel, or stainless with copper bottom. Pure aluminum is an abomination unless it is very thick. Avoid the flimsy Teflon-lined pans with folding handles that are sold in camping shops. I purchase a high-grade, Teflon-lined skillet and replace the plastic handle with a removable one, which I bend from 0.187-inch-diameter spring wire (see Figure 2-1). The mounting bracket for the handle is made from hardware store aluminum flat stock. It secures with two brass bolts that are easily removed when the pan wears out. I also outfit some of my pots with these rigid wire handles.

I recently encouraged Kevin Carr of Chosen Valley Canoe Accessories to make a handle kit for those who don't want to make their own (contact him at 507–867–3961, or e-mail k2carr@aol.com).

Eight-cup coffeepot or kettle. A wide-based kettle heats faster and is less tippy than a coffeepot, and you can pour with one hand. Pack onions, green peppers, cheese, and other crushable/breakables inside your empty kettle.

An oven of some sort. Specialized trail ovens, such as the efficient Bakepacker, are nice, but they're excess baggage on a go-light trip.

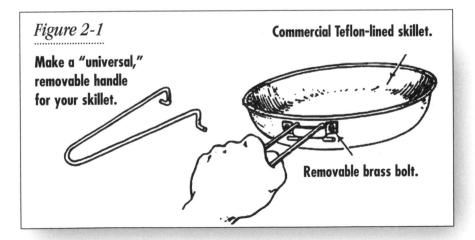

Figure 2-1

Commercial Teflon-lined skillet.

Make a "universal," removable handle for your skillet.

Removable brass bolt.

You can easily improvise a convection oven from existing cookware. Chapter 6, The Art of Baking, shows how.

Two nesting stainless-steel Sierra cups, for use as compact ladles and emergency drinking cups. Steel cups won't warp or melt when you set them on a stove or by the campfire to heat tea.

One nesting bowl per person. Metal bowls are heavy and they transfer heat to your hands. Plastic bowls are cooler and easier to clean. Why doesn't someone make a stainless steel bowl with a removable, heat-resistant plastic bottom? Bowls should be colored or numbered so that each person will always use the same one. This eliminates sharing germs at meals. Keep nested cookware inside a fitted nylon sack.

Individual items. If you want to go light, one metal spoon per person is enough. Gourmet cooks will add a fork. Everyone carries their own knife and insulated mug. Be sure the mug has a fitted cover to keep heat in and heat-seeking insects out. Leash the cover to the mug with a piece of fishing line.

Fabric utensil roll. Buy one from the Duluth Tent & Awning

Company in Minnesota (800-849-4489) or make your own. Be sure the roll has snaps or ties on top, so you can hang it from a clothesline. Chapter 7 shows why.

My utensil roll contains: one plastic pancake turner, one wooden spoon, one rubber spatula, one wooden spatula, one miniature cheese grater, two bamboo tongs, one utility knife (I like the folding carbon-steel "French picnic knife," which costs under $10 at outdoor stores), one tiny wire strainer (1-inch diameter screen) for straining coffee grounds, and four removable wire pot handles.

Spice bag. I carry small containers of nearly every spice known to man. My favorites are cayenne, garlic, cumin, oregano, basil, thyme, lemon pepper, and Old Bay Seasoning. No one will fault you for bringing too many spices on a backwoods camping trip.

Two-quart, graduated plastic pitcher. This is convenient for mixing powdered drinks, pancake mixes, and instant puddings as well as for hauling water to the cooking site.

Dishwashing materials. A four-ounce bottle of liquid detergent, a plastic sponge, and one abrasive and one non-abrasive 3-M nylon scratcher are all you need. I use synthetic chamois towels for drying dishes and mopping up spills.

Dish sterilizing materials. You can sterilize camp dishes by adding a splash of chlorine bleach to the final rinse water. Or add a convenient Effersan tablet. Effersan tablets have 30 percent available chlorine in a handy dry form (Effercept Products, Inc., 800-841-0410).

Insulated cozies for your pots. When it's cold and windy, you'll want insulated fabric cozies, like the ones grandma used to keep her teapot warm. Chapter 7, Cooking Tricks, shows how to make and use cozies. You may want to read this section before you tackle Chapter 3.

One thin-bladed sheath knife with a 4- to 5-inch-long flat-ground blade. Try to spread jam, scrape peanut butter from the bottom of a poly bottle, or slice lunch meat or cheese with a common jackknife or husky "deer skinner" and you'll see why a thin, fixed-blade knife is so important. My favorite trail knife is the "Cliff Knife," which I designed when I couldn't find a suitable replacement for my worn out tool-steel Gerber shorty. It has a wafer-thin, 4.3-inch blade of L6 tool steel and it's custom made by Idaho Knife Works (509-994-9394).

Gasoline stove. Ideally, you should have one burner for every four people. Of course you can cook on a fire (where permitted), but weather frequently makes this impractical.

Breakfasts to Begin the Day

ome years ago, while guiding eight teenagers on a canoe trip in Ontario, I came upon a young couple whose tent was pitched smack dab in the middle of the portage trail. It was early morning, and the day was punctuated by a cold, persistent rain. We'd begun our travel at 3:00 A.M. in the calm of night, hoping to beat the stopper headwinds that usually arise with the sun.

Our traveling fuel for the past five hours had been two Carnation breakfast bars apiece and a couple of beef sticks. The kids were famished. And chilled. We had agreed to stop at the portage (the only flat spot around), build a fire, and cook a wholesome breakfast.

Within minutes after landing, colleague Al Todnem and I had a cheery blaze going and a double rain-tarp strung overhead. Al put the finishing touches on the fly, while I fired up the Two Optimus 111B stoves and began frying bacon. This accomplished, I turned my attention to the "mocoa" (a mixture of coffee and cocoa: kids love it!). The fire was burning nicely, so I set the light stainless grill across two logs and put on the twenty-cup kettle. "Maybe twenty minutes," I mused. "By then, everything will be done."

Back to the stove to give the bacon a stir. Pour off some grease, consolidate the meat into the big skillet. Add a cover to keep in heat. Turn down the flame to simmer.

"How you want your eggs, Angie?"

"Over light," comes the reply.

In a second, skillet two is wiped free of grease with paper toweling packed with the breakfast meal. A teaspoon of vegetable oil is added and the eggs go on. Again, a cover speeds cooking. As the eggs simmer, I check the bacon, then slice a bagel and put each half face down next to the eggs. I salt and pepper the eggs, cover 'em, and relax with a cup of just-brewed mocoa.

Two sips later, the eggs are done. I shovel them into a bowl, squirt the bagel halves with Parkay, and direct Angie to the bacon.

"Next! How ya want your eggs, Tom?"

Total preparation time for this meal—ten people—is just thirty-five minutes. Add another thirty to build and extinguish the fire, warm cold feet, do the dishes, and burn the trash, and we're out in just over an hour.

Warm and well fed? You bet!

Oh yeah, about that couple in the tent. Midway through our meal they struggled, bleary-eyed, into the chilling drizzle, marveled at our setup, and politely asked if they could warm up by the fire. Then they retired to the vestibule of their tent, where they awkwardly heated a small pot of water on their Peak I stove. For breakfast they had tea and instant oatmeal, which they consumed in cold Sierra cups beneath the dripping umbrella of a white pine tree.

They were still sipping tea and looking into the sky for salvation as we trucked down the portage trail. They were ordinary Fords and Chevys; we were the sports cars that just blew past! ⟩

As you can see, outdoor cooking is a whole lot more than menus. Even simple meals are not at all easy to make when the wilderness becomes competitive. Here are my favorite meals to start the day, along with tips for preparing them. These meals require boiling, frying, or simmering. Maximum preparation time for four people is twenty minutes. You'll need one good trail stove or a well-tended fire, plus the "kitchen" suggested in Chapter 2.

Bacon/Eggs/Buttered Bagel with Jam

Bacon. Sliced, sodium nitrite–rich, store-bought bacon will keep at least three days in July heat. Slab (unsliced) bacon may last a week or more. I've kept vacuum-sealed Canadian bacon for ten days. Mold won't grow without air, which is why vacuum-sealing works so well. Most large grocery stores have vacuum-sealing machines and will wrap your meats accordingly, and at no extra charge, if you request.

Try inexpensive Celebrity canned bacon (a product of Hungary) if you can find it. You can also buy pre-cooked, preserved, vacuum-sealed bacon (it's pricey!) in some camping shops.

Eggs. Dried eggs are available at every camp shop and co-op. You can get cholesterol-free dried egg substitutes at supermarket delicatessens. All hype aside, none compare to fresh eggs.

Supermarket eggs may be days or weeks old when you get them. Even so, they'll keep unrefrigerated for at least a week in hot weather. Farm-fresh eggs will last a month if the shells remain intact. Never break eggs into a bottle for easy carrying: once the bacterial barrier (eggshell) is destroyed, they'll spoil immediately.

Tip: **How to carry fresh eggs. Small and medium-size eggs have thicker shells than large eggs and so are less apt to break in transit. Carry eggs in the original containers (cardboard is better than plastic foam). I wrap the cartons with bubble wrap, then lightly vacuum-seal them. I carry the sealed egg cartons on top of my pack. I can't recall when I last broke an egg.**

Bagels. I prefer Lender's raisin bagels for breakfast. The raisins prevent the bagels from drying out, thus increasing unrefrigerated pack life to a full week. Double-bag bagels in plastic or, for real longevity, ask your grocer to vacuum-seal them. Bagels are nearly indestructible.

COOKING PROCEDURE

At home you'd separate bacon strips, lay them flat, and cook them slowly, with plenty of "breathing space." In the woods, you need a more efficient method, especially when you must prepare a lot of bacon for a large crew. Fire up the stove (medium heat) and add bacon all-at-once to a cold pan. Swish it around at the start to get some grease distributed, then immediately cover the pan. Stir the tangled mess frequently. Pour off grease only if it threatens to overflow the pan. The combined deep-fry/cover-steam process will cook one to two pounds of bacon to lightly crisp perfection in less than ten minutes.

To keep cooked bacon hot until you're ready to eat, place it in a covered pot lined with paper toweling. Set the pot on a square of closed-cell foam and snug your down vest over the pot. Better yet, use a fitted "cozy" like the one illustrated in Figure 7-2.

I can't overstress the importance of using fitted covers *and* cozies on all your cooking pots. Low temperatures and a chilling breeze can rob enough heat from pots to prevent uniform cooking. In subzero weather some stoves that are "powerful enough for summer" won't boil water in a covered pot! If you want to keep second servings hot, you'll bring a cozy for every pot.

Eggs. Wipe the bacon skillet clean of grease and bacon scraps before you begin the eggs. Yes, you can cook eggs in bacon grease, but you'll probably burn them. Better to use a clean pan and fresh vegetable oil. A teaspoon of oil is needed in even a Teflon pan. The skillet should be moderately hot.

If your stove puts out too much heat at its lowest setting, use a flame-spreader (a tin can lid works great) between the fire and pan. A pan cover is essential, especially on a windy day.

Bagels. Slice a bagel and squirt each open face with margarine. Then slide the eggs to the edge of the skillet and place each bagel-half face down in the pan. Cover the skillet for fifteen seconds, then quickly add a dash of cold water to the skillet and cover again. Everything will "steam cook" to moist perfection in about twenty seconds. For best results, use a "top cozy" (Figure 7-2) on your skillet cover.

Pita Melt and Egg McPita

Here's a fast-cooking breakfast that's always a hit. You'll need one pita (Mediterranean pocket bread) per person, two or three slices of Canadian or regular bacon, and a slab of good cheese. Plastic bagged pita bread (at most supermarkets and all Greek food stores) keeps at least two weeks in summer. Hard cheeses like Cheddar or Colby may last a month. Just trim away any surface mold that appears.

PREPARATION

Fry the bacon and set it aside. Leave a hint of bacon grease in the skillet. Place an unsliced pita bread into the low-heat skillet, top with thin-sliced or fresh-grated cheese and cooked bacon, and cover for fifteen seconds. Then crack the cover and add a dash of water to the hot skillet. The steam will melt the cheese (it takes less than thirty seconds) and moisten the pita.

Fold the pita bread over, sandwich style, top with salsa, and serve immediately. You can also make an "Egg McPita" by adding a scrambled or over-medium fried egg to the sandwich. You may substitute fried summer sausage, ham, or salami for the bacon.

Garlic Cheese Pita or Garlic Cheese Burrito

Cut pita bread in half and fill the pockets with thin-sliced or grated cheese. Heavily sprinkle garlic powder and oregano (optional) over the cheese. Fry the pita halves in a well-oiled (I prefer olive oil) covered skillet for about twenty seconds. Then flip the pitas and quickly add a dash of cold water to "steam-melt" the cheese. Cook for an additional twenty seconds and serve immediately. So good, it could be a main meal!

Tortillas are less filling than pitas, but they have a more delicate flavor. Fry each tortilla flat in a well-oiled skillet for about ten seconds, then flip it over and add grated cheese and a dash of garlic powder to the lightly toasted side. Quickly roll the tortilla into a burrito shape, add cold water to steam, then cover and simmer for twenty seconds. I serve these as an hors d'oeuvre with chili, pasta dishes, and soup.

Cinnamon Burritos, Brown Sugar-Stewed Apples, and Smoked Pork Sausage

Cinnamon burritos taste like cinnamon rolls. They're big-time favorites!

INGREDIENTS

You'll need (per person): one giant tortilla, three tablespoons brown sugar, ¼ teaspoon cinnamon, dehydrated apples (every supermarket has 'em), liquid margarine, and smoked pork sausage.

Start the stewed fruit and smoked porkies before you begin the burritos. You'll need one pot to boil the sausage, another to boil the fruit. To the fruit, add brown sugar and cinnamon to taste. The fruit will only absorb so much sugar, so there's no need to measure. When the water boils, give the fruit a stir, then remove the pot from the heat and set it on an insulated pad. Add a cozy cover and allow the fruit to stew for ten minutes.

Evenly distribute a generous amount of liquid margarine, brown sugar, and cinnamon on the face of each tortilla. Roll to form burritos. Place burritos folded seam down on a warm pan, lightly oiled with liquid margarine. (You can cook six burritos at a time in a 12-inch skillet.) Cover and fry at low heat for twenty seconds, then turn the burritos (use bamboo tongs) and add a dash of water to steam. Cook for thirty more seconds, then serve.

Can you taste it? A cinnamon-roll burrito, oozing with melted brown sugar and hot cinnamon-flavored margarine, covered with sweet steaming apple slices, served with a side of smoked sausage. Bush breakfasts don't get much better than this!

Luxurious Pancakes

It's pointless to make pancakes or muffins from scratch when so many good mixes are available. Just use Bisquick or your favorite batter and the following tricks of the trade.

1. Disregard the mixing directions. Pour the dry mix into your two-quart plastic pitcher and add water, a little at a time, stirring frequently, until the consistency is moderately runny. The tendency is towards a too-thick mix, which cooks badly in the field. Batter will thickens as it sets; you'll have to thin it again later.

2. Add about two tablespoons (the amount isn't critical) of melted margarine to each six cups of liquid batter. The margarine will make the cakes more flexible and less likely to stick to the pan.

3. Use *medium* heat and just a few drops of cooking oil to fry the first half dozen cakes. It's par for the course to Frisbee the first cake into the fire to get the skillet heat right. Don't attempt to fry several cakes at a time. Instead, limit your accomplishments to one cake per pan. Keep each cake thin and spread it nearly to the skillet edges. Again, a cover speeds cooking.

After the first half dozen pancakes, you can limit use of cooking oil to a few drops every three cakes or so. The margarine in the mix will provide the lubrication you need.

4. Completed cakes are kept hot in a covered pot set near the fire, or use the down vest/tea cozy arrangement explained in Chapter 7.

Tip: **The best commercial pancake mix I've found is Sturdi-wheat, which is made in Red Wing, Minnesota (800-201-9650). It's been around since 1939 but has just recently mushroomed in popularity. Just add water; the batter rises to form a light, bubbly meringue. Sturdiwheat cakes have a light, almost sour-dough taste.**

Meanwhile... pour your cold syrup into a small covered pot and add 50 percent margarine and a dash of cinnamon (optional). Heat to near boiling and set aside. Pancakes will later be smothered with this hot mixture.

Tip: **Try peanut butter as a topping. Sounds awful, but adds a wonderfully rich taste. For a gourmet touch, add a handful of cooked wild rice to the mix. Oh m'God, this is incredible!**

Let's review the tricks: **1)** Batter should be pea soup–thin. **2)** Margarine adds taste to the mix and all but eliminates burning. **3)** One cake per pan is the rule. **4)** Flamboyantly discard the first cake. **5)** Heat syrup and mix half-and-half with margarine, serve on cakes.

Delicious Hot Cereals

Red River Cereal is a nutritious blend of crunchy grains that's served in the best fishing camps in Canada. It cooks to a rich creamy consistency in just five minutes. Most supermarkets have it.

Sturdiwheat hot cereal has a rich taste (the outer wheat layers are left on the grain). Get it from the Sturdiwheat company in Red Wing, Minnesota.

Kashi is a breakfast pilaf made from seven whole grains and sesame. It's a pleasant change from traditional hot cereals.

Old time, slow-cook oatmeal: Instant oatmeal is traditional for fast-moving days when you want to get up and go. But old-fashioned, slow-cook Quaker Oats are much better. Really, now, when did you last have the real thing?

If you want to make these cereals taste grand, add dehydrated fruit bits (you'll find 'em in the dried fruit section of your store) and brown sugar to the cold water before you start cooking. For mouth-watering elegance, include chopped dates and walnuts. Use the cozy system explained in Chapter 7 when you prepare hot cereals.

No cereal is complete without milk, which you'll have to rehydrate from powdered form. Most powdered milk you find in grocery stores tastes awful. Milkman ("with the kiss of cream") is by far the best. It's available only in camping stores. Sanalac, which you'll find at specialty supermarkets, is nearly as good and much less expensive.

Brandy-Stewed Fruit

INGREDIENTS

One package of mixed evaporated fruit, ¼ teaspoon cinnamon, 2 heaping teaspoons of white or brown sugar or honey (you can substitute sugared cherry or apple-flavored drink crystals), and 1 shot of brandy, Yukon Jack, or Southern Comfort.

COOKING PROCEDURE

Place fruit, sugar, cinnamon, liquor, and enough water to cover the fruit into a small pot with tight-fitting cover. Bring to a boil and simmer for fifteen minutes or until fruit is tender. The result will excite the stodgiest crew.

Camp Omelet

INGREDIENTS

eggs

cheese

onion and/or green pepper (optional)

COOKING PROCEDURE

Beat the eggs and pour a thin layer into a hot, greased skillet. Salt and pepper to taste, add diced onion and/or green pepper, and lay thin slices of cheese on top. Cover immediately and cook on low heat for about a minute, then flip half the egg over to sandwich the cheese and veggies inside. Cover and cook another half minute or so. Optional: top with spicy salsa or Cajun hot sauce.

Easy Toast

Set a dry (no cooking oil) skillet on a medium-hot stove or fire. Sprinkle about ¼ teaspoon salt into the skillet and set your bread or bagel-half on top. The bread will toast to a golden brown without burning, and the salt won't stick to the bread.

Tasty Camp Beverages

Use fresh, fine-ground coffee. Bring water to a boil, then remove the pot from the heat. Add one tablespoon of coffee per cup to the pot. Stir once, cover the pot, and set it aside for about three minutes. Some cooks add a dash of cold water to settle the grounds, but this is unnecessary and simply cools the brew.

Tip: **For gourmet coffee, try adding ¼ teaspoon of cinnamon and/or a splash of almond extract to 8 cups of coffee water.**

To make mocoa, use instant cocoa mix and substitute brewed coffee for the hot water. Mocoa-mint flavor results when you add a few drops of peppermint extract to the coffee/cocoa mix. For an interesting alternative, try a splash of peppermint schnapps in your mocoa.

Some cooks add a light pinch of salt and an eggshell to the coffee water. The key to making a great camp coffee is to boil only the water, not the coffee!

Midday Repast

For most Americans, lunch, per se, is more traditional than essential. In the wilderness, however, it is both a time to fuel the body and soothe its aches and senses. Hiking boots are shuffled off and "hot spots" are carefully attended; sweltering brows are wiped with cool, clear water; bodies yawn out full frame for a moment's doze. For the next thirty minutes or so, there is time to relax and appreciate the beauty of God-made things.

Given your present state of mind, the very last thing you want is to toil over a cranky stove, nurse a reluctant fire, cook up a gourmet meal, and afterwards wash and dry the dishes.

Simply put, lunch should be easy. If you can't unwrap it, slice it, spread it, or open a can, forget it. On a really severe day you might cheat and boil some water for tea or instant soup, but basically, you'll bring a cold bag lunch—one prepared back home under the auspices of sound nutrition and good taste.

Hikers, bikers, canoeists, hunters, and fishermen can choose from these time-proven entrees.

Pita Bread

Pita is my mainstay bread for nearly every noon repast. One pita per person is plenty, even on a gut-wrenching, high-altitude hike. Stuff your pocket bread with:

Block cheddar or colby cheese. Avoid soft and sliced cheeses of any kind: these spoil quickly. Processed cheeses (which aren't really cheeses at all) are tasteless and oily. Remember, mold won't grow without air—reason enough to specify vacuum-sealing or a full wax covering.

Sausage or salami which need no refrigeration. "Barrel O'Beef" Cervelat and Summer Sausage keep for weeks in summer heat if the casing is not broken. Figure one-eighth pound per person per meal.

Peanut butter and jam or jelly. Kraft jellies in rugged, squeezable plastic containers are convenient, but canned Canadian Malkin's jam (there are tons of flavors!) is a class act. You can order this delicious jam from Joynes Department Store in Grand Marais, Minnesota (218-387-2233). Joynes also has the wonderful Red Rose tea, which is imported from England. No wilderness trip is complete without an evening cup of Red Rose.

Something salty. The craving for salt intensifies on a long trip. Salted nuts, pretzels, sunflower and pumpkin seeds, and salty snack mixes are lunchtime favorites.

Something sweet. Chocolate nut and wafer bars, classy (expensive) chocolate, and fruit-filled cookies are popular.

Cooking in the Outdoors   **23**

Other lunch ideas. Bagels (raisin and onion varieties stay fresh longest—about three days) granola bars, instant drink mixes (ice tea is most popular), mixed evaporated fruit, fruit breads (banana, pumpkin, date-and-nut), and fruit cakes (they keep forever!). Or try the wonderful Hudson Bay Bread and Northwoods soda bread described in this chapter.

Monster Cookies

INGREDIENTS

3 eggs
1 cup white sugar
1½ cups brown sugar
¼ tablespoon Karo syrup
2 teaspoons baking soda
¾ teaspoon vanilla
¼ pound margarine
¾ pound peanut butter
Shelled, salted peanuts (add what you like)
4½ cups oatmeal
½ pound M&Ms

PREPARATION

Mix in bowl. Drop onto greased cookie sheet (flatten the tops) and bake at 350° Fahrenheit for 12 minutes. Makes about two dozen gigantic cookies.

Hudson Bay Bread

Another complete meal. Hudson Bay Bread is traditional traveling fare in youth camps from Maine to Minnesota and throughout Canada. Charles L. Sommers Canoe Base in Ely, Minnesota, has been serving it to Boy Scouts since 1960. It is rumored that the base got the recipe from the Minnesota Outward Bound School. Hudson Bay Bread is a hands-down favorite on strenuous trips, but it's too rich for snacking at home. There are many variations. This is the "official" recipe, to which I always add chocolate chips. The following recipe makes a ten-day supply for a crew of four.

INGREDIENTS

3 cups soft margarine or butter
4 cups white sugar

⅓ cup light Karo corn syrup
⅔ cup honey
2 teaspoons maple flavoring (Mapleine)
19 cups finely ground rolled oats (not instant oats!)
1½ cups sliced almonds
1 cup chocolate chips

Cream together above ingredients. Gradually add the sliced almonds and chocolate chips and rolled oats. Some cooks also add shredded coconut and raisins.

PREPARATION

Press into greased cake pan about ¼ to ½ inch thick. Bake at 325° Fahrenheit for about 20 minutes, until golden brown. Don't overcook! Press down on the Hudson Bay bread with a spatula (to prevent crumbling) before you cut and remove the squares from the pan. "Scout serving size" (twice what most adults will tolerate) measures 3.5 inches square, so as to fit exactly in protective half-gallon milk cartons. I wrap each square in plastic wrap, then vacuum-seal each day's lunch supply. Shelf life is a full summer or more. Unused bars freeze well and keep till next year.

GORP

An anachronism for "good old raisins and peanuts," there are many variations. Here's my favorite version (add or subtract what you like): Mix approximately equal amounts of M&Ms, raisins, blanched, salted peanuts (not dry-roasted), salted, shelled sunflower seeds, and Cheerios. Spice the concoction with a handful of chopped sugared dates. Great shelf life ... and taste!

Note: **You'll find dozens of recipes for heavy breads and bars in conventional cookbooks. Simply select what strikes your fancy, and don't take the recipe too seriously. You really don't need every ingredient on the list. Even the amounts can be shuffled within reasonable limits. If you don't have "whole wheat flour," substitute white enriched flour. No coconut? Leave it out. And yes, you can make delicious breads, cakes, and biscuits without milk or eggs. Recipes are a guide to good eating, no more. Discover this, and you'll be well on your way to becoming an excellent camp cook.**

Hyacinths for the Soul

After a fast-paced breakfast and determined lunch, supper is hyacinths for the soul. At last there's time to stretch out before a crackling fire and savor a tasty meal and second cup of coffee without concern for self-imposed time constraints or the ambitions of your friends. And later there's corn to pop, brownies or cakes to bake, and flavored teas or hot spiced liquor to drink.

The mealtime gathering embodies all that's right and good about being in a place that's wild and free.

A grand (which need not mean lavish) supper encapsulates the mood of the day and sets a favorable tone for the morrow. A slovenly, tasteless meal evokes the opposite. Fortunately, quality suppers are easy if you adapt these guidelines and proven tricks.

Recipes

As stated in the previous chapter, recipes should not be taken literally. Seldom do you need every item, in the amounts indicated. Cakes, for example, usually call for eggs—something you can omit on the trail and not miss at all. White sugar can be substituted for brown; or use honey, Karo, or maple syrup. In a pinch, try flavored, sweetened drink crystals. Need to stretch a meat, rice, or pasta dish? Just add some instant soup, potato buds, or Bisquick dumplings to the mix. And don't be afraid to mix flavors, say chicken-vegetable soup and beef stew. Imagination, and a willingness to experiment is the key to successful trail meals.

Spices

The blandest trail meal becomes king's fare when artfully spiced. On canoe trips, where space and weight allows for some extras, I bring every spice on the planet. For go-light adventures, I carry salt, pepper, garlic flakes, and an "all spice" that consists of approximately equal amounts of the following ingredients:

seasoned salt (I buy a commercial blend)

oregano

marjoram

dash of thyme

dash of onion powder

Mix the above ingredients and pack them inside a 35mm film container.

Preparations

Field rations usually contain three basic parts: pasta or rice, meat or TVP (textured vegetable protein), and veggies. Need more food value in a given meal? Just add elbow macaroni, noodles, Minute Rice, or cheese. Stretch vegetable components with dried soups or mixed vegetables. Add dehydrated hamburger to stews, soups and rice and pasta dishes. Or throw in diced, fried sausage, canned shrimp or crab, or chunk white chicken. Here again, creativity pays rich dividends.

The Raman/cheese hamburger soup exemplifies this principle. It's one of my favorite trail meals.

Raman/Cheese Hamburger Soup *(serves 4)*

INGREDIENTS

4 packs of Raman noodles. Or substitute a favorite dry soup mix. Double the suggested package servings on the soup to yield 8 servings.

1 pound (fresh weight) of dehydrated hamburger, or substitute ½ pound of diced/fried salami or two 5-ounce cans of chunk white chicken. For another alternative, try chicken-vegetable soup with chunk white chicken or canned shrimp.

½ cup of dried shiitake mushrooms

2-inch cube of cheese (optional)

If you're using soup instead of Raman, bring a handful of wide egg noodles, kluski, or spaetzel (spaetzel won't break in your pack).

¼ onion or ½ tablespoon of minced, dried onion flakes (optional)

dash of your special "all-spice"

1 bouillon cube, beef or chicken (adds richness)

dash of cayenne pepper

PREPARATION

Make the soup according to package directions but add 20 percent more water. Add everything but the noodles at the start of cooking. When the water boils, toss in the noodles. Simmer 5 minutes or "cozy up" and set aside for 15 minutes (see Chapter 7). Cut the cheese into thin strips and stir in just before serving. Delicious!

Dumpling soup is another easy trail meal based on the same principle.

Dumpling Soup *(serves 4)*

INGREDIENTS

Instant minestrone, vegetable, beef-vegetable or chicken soup (double suggested serving amounts to yield 8 servings)

⅔ cup of uncooked Minute Rice

⅔ cup of Bisquick

pinch of your secret all-spice

handful of dehydrated hamburger or a half cup of chipped/dried beef (optional)

If you're using a chicken soup base, supplement with 1 can of chunk-white chicken or a package of freeze-dried chicken. Gourmet Award is the best tasting chicken soup base I've found. Use it like bouillon; no refrigeration necessary.

PREPARATION

Add 20 percent more water than called for in the directions. Failure to do this will produce glue, not stew! Add meats and spices to the cold water. Bring to a boil, add Minute Rice, then drop marble-sized dumplings into the brew. Simmer about 5 minutes, until dumplings are done. Here again, you can add cheese at the last moment or beef up with fried sausage or canned meats.

Tip. **To make dumplings (or biscuits) without soiling your hands, pour batter and water into a plastic Ziploc bag. Seal the bag and knead the contents until they are well mixed. When the consistency is correct, punch a hole in the bag bottom and squeeze the mix—use the bag like a cake decorator—into the soup (or your oven).**

Chowder *(serves 4 to 6)*

Chowders are tasty and easy to make. This recipe was suggested by my friend Bob Dannert.

3 cups dehydrated hashbrown potatoes

potato buds: enough to make 2 quarts of cooked potatoes

1 fresh onion, or substitute ¼ cup of dehydrated flakes

1 tablespoon green pepper flakes

handful of dried mushrooms (optional)

handful dried corn, peas or other vegetables—be imaginative

three packs (each pack makes 1 quart) of Milkman instant milk mix

fresh-caught fish (or substitute canned shrimp or crab)

PREPARATION

Place everything except Potato Buds and fish into your largest pot. Add sufficient water to rehydrate the mix and make a slushy soup. Bring to a boil, stirring frequently, then add enough Potato Buds to thicken the brew to the consistency you like. Or thin with water, as you prefer. Salt and pepper to taste.

When the chowder is cooked, add 1-inch chunks of raw fish to the lightly boiling brew. Cook 5 full minutes (to kill any tapeworm parasites), no more, and serve immediately. Makes about 12 cups.

Tip: **For a great taste treat, add raw fish chunks (boil 5 minutes) to any instant soup mix.**

Classy Spaghetti *(serves 3 to 4)*

First-rate spaghetti is a class act in the wilderness, and it's easy to make. Here's my recipe.

INGREDIENTS

1 packet of Schilling (or other) spaghetti sauce

1 small onion (or 1 tablespoon minced, dried onion) will suffice for up to 8 servings

½ small, green pepper. Or substitute ½ teaspoon dried pepper flakes

dash of dried celery flake

1 6-ounce can of tomato paste. Note: Tomato paste (and prepared spaghetti sauce) may be reduced to an easily rehydrated "leather" in any food dehydrator

dash of your "all spice"

vermicelli (cooks faster than regular spaghetti; I use one pound for each 4 to 5 people)

dehydrated hamburger: ¼ pound per person (or substitute fried, diced summer sausage, salami, Canadian bacon, or canned ham. All these meats work well.)

1 small can of mushrooms (dried mushrooms are very good) for each 4 to 10 people

dash of coarsely ground red pepper

1 tablespoon Parmesan cheese per serving

2 tablespoons olive oil

½ cup green or black olives

PREPARATION

Fill your largest pot with water, add a dash of salt and a tablespoon of olive oil, heat and turn your attention to making the sauce.

Place sauce ingredients, spices, meat, coarsely cut vegetables and 2 teaspoons of olive oil, plus 2 quarts of cold water (more or less) into a covered, medium pot. Bring to a boil, stirring frequently. Then, turn off the stove and set the pot on a square of closed-cell foam. Cover the pot with an insulated cozy so cooking will continue for 20 more minutes.

Bring a second pot of lightly salted water to a boil and add full-length vermicelli to the boiling water. Stir for 1 minute, then remove the pot from the heat and "cozy up." The pasta is done when it is slightly firm *(al dente)*—about 20 minutes.

30

Tip: **Making spaghetti with full-length strands is a class act. Spaghetti strands won't break if you vacuum-seal them, as suggested on page 6. Again, don't waste stove fuel cooking pasta and sauce. Use the cozy system explained in Chapter 7.**

Don't attempt to drain pasta water. A mess invariably results. Instead, pluck noodles from the pot with a fork and spoon.

Pour a little olive oil into the pasta water to keep the noodles from sticking.

For low-class mushy spaghetti (genuine camping food!), break up the vermicelli into small pieces and cook everything (pasta and sauce) in one pot at one time. Your guests won't be impressed, but it's fast and easy.

Super Chili for Four

Good hot chili is the meal of choice on a cold, wet day. There's no right or wrong way to make chili. Vary components and water amounts to suit your fancy. It's almost impossible to ruin chili.

INGREDIENTS

1 package of your favorite chili mix (I buy a spicy hot, high-grade mix.)

1 medium can of stewed or chopped tomatoes (provides texture)

½ cup *(or more)* of tomato powder (Or bring canned tomato paste if you can afford the space and weight. For decidedly inferior chili, substitute four envelopes of Lipton's tomato Cup-A-Soup for the entire tomato component.)

1 coarsely chopped, small onion (or substitute 1 tablespoon of onion flakes)

⅓ coarsely cut green pepper, or a ½ teaspoon of dried pepper flakes

1 16-ounce can of kidney or chili beans (I use dehydrated canned beans)

1 pound fresh or dehydrated hamburger (or use diced, fried salami— it's spicy, so be frugal—Canadian bacon, canned ham or TVP.)

1 cup elbow macaroni or spaghetti broken into 2-inch lengths

¼ teaspoon cumin powder

salt and pepper to taste, plus a shot of your "all spice"

ground red pepper (lots of it!)

3-inch chunk of cheddar cheese (optional)

Toss everything, except the tomato powder and macaroni, into
your largest pot along with 2 quarts of water. Bring to a boil, then
slowly add tomato powder until you get a medium-thick chili. Then
add the macaroni and stir for 30 seconds. Remove the pot from the
heat and "cozy up" for 20 minutes. Stir before serving and mix in a
few 1-inch chunks of cheddar cheese. Good stuff!

Northwoods Stir-Fry *(serves 4)*

Scenario: First night on a wilderness campout. You want to wow
your friends with a gourmet supper of grilled filet mignon, rice
topped with fried mushrooms and gravy, and a fresh salad. (See
Chapter 7 for the logistics of carrying fresh fruits and vegetables.)
Problem is, the weather won't cooperate. Rain is coming in sheets
and everyone has miserably retired to their tents.

Everyone but you, that is. Your mission is to fulfill your promise to
feed the crew a luscious meal.

At the outset, you'll have to rig a rainfly to get out of the weather. My
books *Camping's Top Secrets* and *Basic Essentials: Camping* will show
you how. However, even with overhead protection, grilling steaks in a
determined rain is, at best, awkward, and frying them is a ruination of
good meat. The answer is to forget about campfires for now and instead
concentrate on making northwoods stir-fry on your stove. The
ingredients at hand include:

4 mouthwatering 8-ounce tenderloin fillets

1 head of lettuce

1 tomato

1 green pepper

1 fresh onion

1 can of mushrooms

2¼ cups of Minute Rice

cooking oil

small plastic bottle of salad dressing

PROCEDURE

Place a friend in charge of making the salad. He/she gets the
lettuce and tomato only. You keep the rest. To eliminate dirtying a
pot, make the salad in a plastic poly bag. Add dressing and shake.

Cooking in the Outdoors   **33**

Fire up your stove(s). First, put on the teapot and prepare a round of Hot Buttered Yukon Jack (recipe follows) to brighten up the crew. In this chilling rain, a hot toddy served with a twinkling smile will establish your expertise as camp cook.

Meanwhile... Slice steak, pepper, and onion into bite-sized strips, and pile them in a small pot. This accomplished, put on the water for Minute Rice. If you have just one stove, you'll need to shuttle pots as follows:

1. Teapot goes on first—requires about 10 minutes to boil.

2. Remove hot teapot: your assistant serves hot Jack while you put on water for Minute Rice—about 8 minutes to boil.

3. Remove boiled Minute Rice water, add rice and set the covered pot aside. If the weather is cold, cover the pot with your sweater or down vest or use a pot cozy to keep contents hot.

4. Pour a few tablespoons of cooking oil into the skillet, warm it slightly, then toss in the meat, stirring frequently as you fry. When meat is half done, add the vegetables and mushrooms. Salt and pepper to taste and sauté 8 to 10 minutes until everything is done. Serve over a bed of rice (inept cooks will mix everything together) with a salad side dish.

As soon as the main meal is off the stove, refill the teapot and put it on again, this time to make cinnamon or amaretto coffee (recipe is in Chapter 3), which will be done 10 minutes later.

Eat and enjoy... laugh at the weather. Your total preparation time is about 30 minutes.

Hoover Curry *(serves 4)*

Named for the Hoover Wilderness Area in the Sierras, this scrumptious recipe was refined by Mickey McBride, a whitewater canoeing fanatic and ardent mountain roamer.

1 tablespoon curry powder

1 pinch red pepper

1 teaspoon dry minced garlic

¼ cup dried onion flakes

2 cups Minute Rice

1 package Knorr leek soup mix

3 to 4 ounces golden raisins

1 5-ounce can chunk white chicken or 1 package freeze-dried
chicken

PREPARATION

Combine all ingredients except the chicken in a Ziploc bag at
home (if using freeze-dried chicken, it's best to add 2 teaspoons of
dry chicken broth to the mix.) To prepare, bring 5 cups water to
boil, stir in ingredients and simmer 10 minutes, stirring
occasionally. If sticking occurs, add a little more water. Serve with
freeze-dried peaches.

For more than 4 people or for a gourmet touch, serve with
Knorr Hot and Sour soup.

Pita Pizza for Four

This is, by far, everyone's favorite meal.

INGREDIENTS

One or two pieces of pita bread per person

½ cup dried tomato powder

⅓ pound fresh mozzarella cheese (hard, fresh cheese keeps nearly a
month if it's vacuum sealed)

oregano

garlic powder

salt

cayenne pepper

basil

Suggested toppings: pepperoni, summer sausage, hard salami,
Canadian bacon, fresh onion, green pepper, black olives, canned
mushrooms, anchovies, smoked oysters, etc.

PROCEDURE

1. Slice and fry the meat and drain off the grease on paper
toweling. Thickly dice the vegetables and mushrooms, fry them
in light oil, then drain off the grease and set them aside.

2. To make the pizza sauce, pour ½ cup of tomato powder into a
bowl and add water to make a thick paste. Sprinkle on oregano,
garlic, basil, salt, and cayenne.

3. Fry an unsliced pita at low heat in a well-oiled, covered skillet. When the bottom of the pita is brown (about 20 seconds), flip it over and thickly spread on tomato sauce, cheese, cooked meat, and toppings to taste. Immediately add a dash of water (to steam-melt the cheese) and cover the pan. Allow the pizza to cook at very low heat for 30 seconds or until the cheese has melted. The result is beyond terrific!

Garlic-Clam Linguini *(serves 8)*

I adapted this recipe from an elegant garlic-clam linguini entree that a friend of mine serves in her Italian restaurant. My crews think it's a knock-out.

INGREDIENTS

4 cans minced clams

1 pound Monterey Jack cheese

1 tablespoon dried parsley

¼ cup olive oil

⅛ pound margarine or olive oil

2 pounds linguini

4 cloves fresh garlic or garlic flakes

heavy dash of basil

1 small onion (optional)

PROCEDURE

Dice onion, garlic, and basil and sauté in olive oil for about 2 minutes. Stir in margarine. Add minced clams (juice and all). Continue to gently sauté for about 5 minutes. Add parsley and continue to cook at low heat in occasionally covered skillet for about 5 minutes.

Meantime, prepare linguini in another pot. Use the cozy system explained in Chapter 7.

When linguini is nearly done (20 minutes), slice the cheese and add it to the clam skillet. Cook slowly and stir vigorously until all cheese is melted.

Pour off water from linguini and quickly toss cooked clam mixture over the linguini. Coat linguini thoroughly. Sprinkle ground black pepper on top and serve immediately.

Tip: **Serve garlic/cheese tortillas as an appetizer.**

Camp Toddies

After a tough day afield, the traditional hot toddy hits the spot. It can be prepared with any whiskey or liquor, though Yukon Jack, Southern Comfort, and Pusser's rum taste best.

Combine the following ingredients in an insulated mug:

1 shot of whiskey

1 teaspoon sugar

dash of cinnamon

pat of margarine

Add boiling water and stir. Superb! Try substituting hot apple-flavored Kool-Aid or cinnamon tea for the boiling water.

Fast Ways to Fix Tasty Fish

Tripod Fish

Old-time woodsmen often used this method to cook large fish without dirtying pots and pans.

Run a cord through the mouth/gills of a gutted (but not scaled or skinned) fish and hang the fish from a lashed tripod. Build a roaring fire beneath the fish. The skin will blacken in the flames but the inner flesh will cook up chalky white. The meat is done when you can flake it with a fork (about 15 minutes). Remove the tripod and fish, squirt the meat with lime or lemon juice, salt to taste, and go at it. Mmm good!

Trapper Planked Fish

Early trappers used this method in the days before aluminum reflector ovens. All you need is a narrow board.

Clean the fish, cut off the head, and split the body along the back. It will look like an open book. Then peg the split fish to the board and set it before a roaring fire. The meat is done when it's white and flaky. If possible, use hardwoods when baking before an open fire. Some soft-woods, such as pine and spruce, contain resins that make fish taste bad.

Sizzlin' Pickerel

Canadian fishing guides prepare this traditional shore lunch in a black iron skillet over a roaring fire. Walleye pike (also called pickerel) and lake trout are the preferred fish species, but any fish that's large enough to fry will do.

Pat-dry clean fillets on paper toweling, then shake them in a plastic bag filled with Bisquick that has been seasoned with salt and lemon pepper. Fry in sizzling hot peanut oil until each side is golden brown (about 5 minutes). For a real treat, sauté some diced onion in the pan before you fry, and/or sprinkle the sizzling fillets with Old Bay or Cajun seasoning. Better yet, bread fish in a fifty-fifty mix of Tony Chachere's Creole Seasoned Fry All (see Cajun Cooking, page 40) and Bisquick.

Steamin' Cakes Alive!

You fried too much fish for supper. What can you do with the leftovers? Save them and make fish cakes for breakfast! Munch on cold cakes for lunch! Cooked leftover fish will keep fine overnight if you store it in a Ziploc bag and keep the bag in a cool place. Refrigeration isn't necessary because the parasites have been killed by cooking. This recipe comes from naturalist Tom Anderson, Director of Lee and Rose Nature Center in Minnesota.

¾ cup milk

1 egg (fresh or dehydrated)

½ small onion, finely chopped

dash of pepper

about 1 teaspoon salt

2 cups cooked fish (any kind)

3 or 4 heaping tablespoons instant mashed potatoes (optional)

Mix all the ingredients, except the fish. Mash the fish with a fork and add it a little at a time to make a thick paste. For great flavor and thicker cakes, add a few tablespoons of instant mashed potatoes to the mix.

Mash the cakes flat and fry 'em in hot oil, like pancakes. Shortly after you flip them over, add a dash of cold water to the pan and cover the pan. This will steam the cakes and make them soft and moist.

Fresh fish tastes great no matter how you fix it, so there's no need to follow these recipes closely. Leave out ingredients you don't like. Under- or overcooking fish is your biggest concern. Remember, your fish is done right when the meat flakes easily with a fork.

Lotsa Matzo Possibilities

Matzo meal is a flour used to make unleavened matzos—a popular flat cracker that looks like hem-stitched cardboard. It's available at Jewish delicatessens and most supermarkets.

Traditional matzo-ball (dumpling) soup is easily made in the field by adding one onion, a dash of celery flake, and a hint of tomato (if you have it) to one ounce of soup base for each five cups of boiling water. Drop golf-ball sized matzo balls into the brew; add a handful of wide egg noodles (optional), and you have a 20 minute treat that you'll relish at home. For a pleasant change, try matzo meal in other soups too.

Fried matzos is another unique dish that's easy to make in the field. Just dip slabs of matzos into a salt and peppered beating egg mixture and fry until golden brown. Top with syrup or brown sugar. Matzos is inexpensive and it keeps for months on the trail.

Cajun Cooking

Yes, you can have genuine Cajun meals in the bush. Packets of gumbo and jambalaya come complete with seasoning and rice and are available by mail from these companies:

Tony Chachere's Creole Foods
P.O. Box 1687
533 North Lombard Street
Opelousas, LA 70571-1687
Phone: 800-551-9066

Oak Grove Smokehouse
17618 Old Jefferson Highway
Prairieville, LA 70769
Phone: 504-673-6857

Gumbo and jambalaya cook up in 20 minutes. Add the recommended amount of water, include an onion, tomato and green pepper, and a can or three of shrimp or crab, plus a generous dash of Tony Cachere's famous Creole Seasoning, and you'll have fare fit for a king.

Always Keep in Mind

Let's review what we've learned about

preparing suppers in the outdoors:

1. Don't take recipes too seriously. More or less—or omission

   of—selected ingredients will seldom spoil the stew.

2. You can substitute similar foods for one another without

   seriously affecting flavor.

3. Increase nutritional value of meals by adding Minute Rice,

   pasta, instant mashed potatoes, or soups.

4. Use spices willingly.

5. Don't believe the servings information on the package.

   The average adult needs about 14 ounces of cooked food

   per meal (more, in strenuous conditions) to retain body

   weight. I always double suggested servings amounts.

6. Don't be afraid to experiment.

The
Art of Baking

I t used to be that only seasoned woodsmen who understood the nuance of yeast breads and well-regulated campfires could prepare mouth-watering baked goods in the outdoors. Everyone else just watched in awe, content to eat their high-energy crackers and whatever they could boil on their gasoline stoves.

Now, advancements in foods technology (there's an instant mix for everything) and cookware have made it possible for anyone to produce perfect cakes and biscuits every time. All you need is a prepared mix, a source of flame (stove or fire), and one of the commercial or jury-rigged ovens suggested below. Here's the procedure.

Baking on an Open Fire

Reflector Oven Method

Baked goods are set on the well-greased shelf of the oven, which is placed before a roaring fire. The key here is *roaring,* as the bright aluminum reflector needs high flames for even heating of upper and lower surfaces. If you can't maintain a hot, bright fire, forget about using this appliance!

Reflector ovens were popular a half-century ago when large campfires were the norm. Today, small fires—or no fires—are the rule, so the bulky reflector is out of place. Nonetheless, reflector baking is easy and fun. And because your food is always visible (not hidden in an enclosed oven), you can take immediate action to prevent burning before it occurs.

PROCEDURE

Set the oven about 8 inches away from the roaring flames (Figure 6-1). You may have to elevate the fire base (on rocks or logs) slightly to ensure even heating. Baking times are about the same as your home oven.

You'll need a long-handled metal spatula to shuffle the buns during the baking process, and a can of Bon-Ami to keep the aluminum surfaces bright. When not in use, fold your oven flat and store it in a protective fabric bag. Where can you get a reflector oven? Try camping shops or your local Boy Scout supply center.

Figure 6-1

Reflector oven baking is easy.

Figure 6-2

Baking a bannock.

Baking in a Skillet—The Traditional Bannock

A bannock is a bread which is baked before an open fire in a large, straight-sided skillet. It can be as simple or complicated as you like. I usually start with a stiff Bisquick dough, then add whatever's on hand—raisins, dehydrated fruit, cinnamon, sugar, honey, or all of the above. Fold in what you like, in the amount you like.

PROCEDURE

Spread the dough, about an inch thick, right to the edges of a well-greased frying pan. Then, set the skillet on ash-covered coals (avoid flame) for a few minutes and slowly cook the bottom of the bannock, occasionally shuffling the pan to prevent burning.

When the bottom of the bannock is golden brown, build the fire high and prop the frying pan about forty-five degrees to the leaping flames (Figure 6-2). Occasionally rotate the skillet (or bannock) until the entire surface of the bread turns a delectable golden brown. Test for doneness with a sliver of wood shaved with your pocket knife. Add a topping of honey and margarine and you'll consume the bannock in one sitting, ashes and all!

The aluminum or stainless steel Dutch oven in which you prepare stews and soups at home is a far cry from the proud artifact which bears the name. A genuine Dutch oven is made of pure ³⁄₁₆-inch thick or heavier, cast iron or aluminum. Several short legs at the base keep hot coals from touching the pot bottom, and a rimmed (deep dish) cover supports a glowing fire on top (Figure 6-3). In a traditional Dutch oven, you can bake, boil, or fry with equal aplomb.

Your best source of old-fashioned, round Dutch ovens is a Boy Scout supply center or mail order catalog that caters to horse wranglers and big game hunters. Cast-iron ovens cook best, but they are terribly heavy and awkward to carry. Aluminum models, though lighter, are just as bulky. One lightweight unit that bakes well and packs compactly is the "Woody" Dutch oven. Made of ³⁄₁₆-inch cast aluminum, two sizes are offered: 6½ inches by 9 inches (3 pounds), and 9 inches by 9 inches (6 pounds). Each oven section may be used separately as a griddle. These high-quality units are available from Woody's Outdoor Cookware, 27 North Hobart Road, Hobart, Indiana 46342; 1–800–82WOODY.

Figure 6-3

The "Woody" Dutch oven.

Figure 6-4

You can make a Dutch oven from any pot and lid.

Using the Dutch oven: A new cast iron oven must be "seasoned" to prevent sticking and burning of foodstuffs. The recommended method is to coat the pot with cooking oil then place it, sans food, in a 350° Fahrenheit oven for an hour or so (same as breaking in a cast iron skillet). Or you can eliminate this folderol and use the oven as is, knowing full well that your first efforts will be imperfect. Aluminum Dutch ovens do not need to be seasoned to prevent sticking or burning.

A well-seasoned oven needs very little grease. A few drops of cooking oil, evenly spread with paper toweling, is enough. Place dough in the oven bottom—a 2-inch thickness is about right. Cover the unit and set it over, but not touching, hot coals.

Tip: **If your Dutch oven does not have legs, cover the coals with ashes to insulate them from the pot bottom. Fill the depression in the oven cover with glistening coals, or build a hot fire on top. Occasionally turn the oven and rotate the cover to ensure even heating. Since the vast majority of heat is applied to the oven top, there's little chance of burning the bread inside.**

Note: **You can easily make an acceptable Dutch oven by inverting a large frying pan over a smaller one, or by placing a skillet, cake pan, or inverted cover on top of a pot (Figure 6–4). However, the thin aluminum construction of this makeshift appliance suggests that you use almost no heat on the bottom (set the oven in the warm ashes). A small, hot fire on top should provide nearly all the heat for baking.**

Baking on a Trail Stove

The Triple-Pan Method

You'll need two nesting skillets (or one skillet and an aluminum pie tin), a high cover, and a half dozen small nails or stones (Figure 6-5).

1. Evenly scatter the nails or stones onto the bottom surface of the large skillet.

2. Place your bread or biscuits into the small frying pan or pie tin and set it on top of the nails (the air space that separates the two pans will prevent burning).

3. Cover the unit and place it on your stove. Use the lowest possible heat setting.

Warning: **Don't use a thin aluminum pan on the bottom: You'll burn a hole right through it!**

Tip: **You can use the triple-pan oven over an open fire, too!**

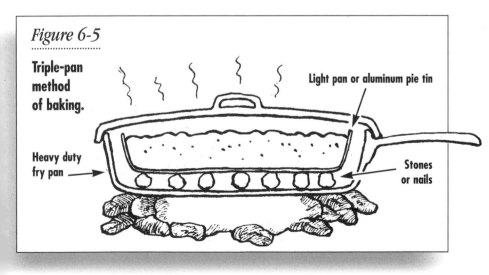

Figure 6-5

Triple-pan method of baking.

Light pan or aluminum pie tin

Heavy duty fry pan

Stones or nails

Figure 6-6

Jell-O mold oven.

Jell-O Mold Oven

All you need is a large-ring aluminum Jell-O mold (about $3.00 at most discount stores) and a high cover. To use the Jell-O mold for baking on your stove:

1. Grease the mold and pour your bake stuff into the outside ring. Decrease the suggested amount of water by up to 25 percent for faster baking.

2. Bring the stove to its normal operating temperature, then reduce the heat to the lowest possible blue-flame setting. Center the Jell-O mold over the burner head (Figure 6-6), top it with a high cover (essential to provide room for the bread to rise), and relax. Heat goes up through the chimney of the mold, radiates off the cover, and cooks from the top, with no chance of burning.

3. Cool the mold by setting it in a shallow pan of water for a few moments.

Important: Even a light breeze will cause uneven heating of the Jell-O mold, resulting in a cake that has one side burned and one side raw. So rotate the mold frequently to distribute heat evenly. A windshield of some sort is essential when using a Jell-O mold oven.

Tip: **Large-burner stoves like the Coleman Peak 1 and double-burner models may burn the edges of the bake stuff. An electric stove burner shield—available for a few dollars at most supermarkets—will eliminate this problem. Simply place the shield under the Jell-O mold. The air space between the shield and mold bottom will prevent burning. The large-size burner shield will fit large-ring Jell-O molds perfectly.**

Baking With Sterno

Scenario: You're camping in an area where fires aren't permitted. You'd like to bake some biscuits but your stove is tied up making supper. How can you utilize your Jello-O mold oven?

Easy. Fire the Jell-O mold with a small (2⅝-ounce) can of Sterno (Don't use the large can: it puts out too much heat!).

Place the can in the center of the ring mold and cover the oven. The Sterno needs oxygen to burn, so you must ventilate the mold by raising it slightly (prop it on a pair of ½-inch diameter sticks). Ventilate the oven cover by cracking it about ⅛ inch.

Recipes

I suggested earlier that it's hard to beat the prepared mixes available at your supermarket. There are two exceptions: Northwoods soda bread and genuine sourdough. Here are the working recipes.

Northwoods Soda Bread

This is one of the best trail breads around. One slice is a complete meal.

INGREDIENTS

4 cups flour

1 teaspoon baking soda

1 tablespoon baking powder

¾ teaspoon salt

2 tablespoons sugar

1¼ cups raisins or chopped sugared dates

1 beaten egg

1 cup buttermilk or sour milk (milk can be soured by adding
   1 tablespoon vinegar or lemon juice per cup of milk)

1 cup unflavored yogurt or sour cream

PREPARATION

Knead it all and bake at medium heat (350° Farenheit in your home oven) for about an hour. Note: This bread is easily made in the field by substituting dried sour cream for the real thing and vinegar-soured Milkman drink mix for the buttermilk. The basic recipe is foolproof: I've substituted brown sugar for white, added jam and cinnamon to the mix, eliminated the eggs and used reconstituted non-fat dry milk instead of yogurt. It is always excellent!

Traditional Sourdough

When I was a forester in eastern Oregon in the mid 1960s, I maintained a sourdough bucket and made biscuits or pancakes several times a week. It's easy. This basic recipe will get you started.

MAKING THE STARTER

Put about 2 cups of flour, 1 tablespoon sugar and ½ cake of yeast into a stone crock or plastic bucket with a loose-fitting lid. Add enough warm water to make a pancake-thick batter. Let the mixture sit at room temperature about three days, until it "sours."

To make bread or biscuits, remove about 1 cup of well-stirred batter and place it in a mixing bowl. To keep the unused mix from over-souring, replace the batter you take with fresh flour and water.

Add about ¼ teaspoon baking soda (the secret is in the soda—don't add too much!). Mix thoroughly. A chemical change will occur and the mixture will bubble up into a meringue-like fluff. Add a dash of salt, about a tablespoon of sugar to taste (don't add too much!), a little melted shortening, and enough flour to make a stiff dough. Make a stiff "working" dough for bread or rolls; thin it out for pancakes.

Force the dough into your awaiting oven; relax, and contemplate one of the great taste sensations in life. Sourdough, as everyone knows, also makes the best pancakes.

Note: **You can keep sourdough for years if you keep diluting it with fresh flour and water. The mix will over-sour (possibly "explode," or ooze out of your bucket), if you don't use it and dilute it on a regular basis. Refrigerating the working mix stops the chemical reaction. Sourdough can be dried and stored and used to start a new mix.**

Tip: **I am indebted to Scott Power for the following tips, which I discovered in his book, *Cooking the Sourdough Way*. When Scott graduated from high school, he and a friend wintered in Dr. Bill Forgey's log cabin near Hudson Bay. Scott—a superb wilderness chef—developed a wealth of scrumptious sourdough recipes, which you'll want to try.**

1. Don't store sourdough in an aluminum pot: A chemical reaction will occur that will adversely affect the flavor. Stainless steel and stoneware are okay.

2. Butter or margarine has better flavor than cooking oil.

3. The most convenient way to carry sourdough on the trail is to mix half a cup of starter with flour until you get a soft ball. Roll the ball in more flour and store it in a plastic bag half filled with flour. This should keep a week or more.

Cooking Tricks

You'd think that culinary skill at home would translate to equal competence afield. Not always. That's because nature frequently doles out stoppers like rain, high winds, darkness, snow, crowded working conditions, canoe upsets, wet firewood, and unsafe water. Why rough it when, with a few tricks, meal preparation can be smoothed to a simple task? The following pages will show you how.

Packing Suggestions

Scenario: It's twilight and misting when, after ten hours of hiking, you arrive at your wilderness base camp. Hastily, you pitch a rain tarp while friends see to the tents. First order of business is a rejuvenating supper of "Classy Spaghetti." Thoughts race through your mind as you search for the ingredients:

Hmmm… got the spaghetti, but where's the tomato paste? Ahhh, got it! "Hey, you guys, anybody seen the dried hamburger? Where's the Parmesan cheese?"

Last thing you need now is to search for things. Everything for the meal should be immediately at hand, all packed in one bag. This you should have done at home!

To save weight and bulk, remove all unnecessary cardboard and paper packaging from foodstuffs before you go afield. Repack pre-measured amounts of "flowable solids" like sugar and Bisquick inside

Ziploc bags. For added security against punctures, place each Ziploc into a color-coded cloth bag. A masking tape label will tell you what's inside. *Important:* Don't forget to include the preparation directions with each entree or ingredient.

Breakable and crushable items such as crackers, cheese, candy bars and fruit should be packed inside rigid cardboard containers or your coffeepot. I use cut-down half gallon milk cartons, which double as emergency fire-starters.

Liquids are best carried in plastic bottles that have screw caps (Figure 7-1). Genuine Nalgene bottles—available at most camping shops—are by far the best. High-grade plastic 1500 milliliter medical IV bottles, which contain "sterile water for irrigation," are also superb. Hospitals discard them after a single use. Ask your doctor to save some for you. Plastic bottles with pop-tops and flip-tops, like those which contain pancake syrup and cooking oil, usually leak. I melt these tops shut in the flame of a gas stove.

Figure 7-1
Nalgene bottles and 1500 ml IV bottle.

Nalgene bottle   1500 ml IV bottle   Nalgene bottle with leash

When packaging each meal, fold over the sharp corners of foil packages so they won't cut through the adjacent plastic bags.

Tips: **1. Sorting meals will be easier if you package them in color-coded nylon bags. I use green for breakfasts, blue for lunches, and red for suppers. Everything for a given meal goes in the bag.**

2. Pack a few sheets of paper toweling with each meal to serve as dish towels. Toilet paper—the Boy Scouts call it "AP" (all purpose) paper—also makes acceptable toweling. Please burn or pack out used toweling and packaging.

Food Preparation Ideas

Cozy Tricks

It's a cold, blustery day, and you're preparing oatmeal for six. You pour Quaker flakes into the boiling water and stir to mix. Then, you cover the pot and adjust the heat to simmer, with hopes the gruel won't burn. Fifteen minutes later you stir and taste. As expected, one bite is raw, the next is burned, and there's a hard black spot glued to the pot bottom. Better eat fast; seconds won't stay hot for long! And thank goodness you don't have to do the dishes.

Try this instead: make insulated "cozies" for your cooking pots from cotton-quilted material or insulated ironing board fabric. A two-piece cozy—top hat and belly band—is better than a one-piece model because the wide band insulates the pot sides when you remove the cover to stir. The skirted top hat can also be used (skirt up) alone on top of a skillet when frying fish or bacon.

HERE'S HOW TO USE YOUR COZY *(Figure 7-2)*

1. Velcro the band tightly around the pot before you begin cooking. Position the bottom of the band half an inch above the bottom of the pot, so the band won't scorch when the stove runs full blast.

2. Measure water for the meal into the pot. Then, cover the pot and put on the "cozy cap." If you're making a freeze-dried or dehydrated entree, add meat, spices, and vegetables to the water. Don't add sauce mix, rice, cereal, or pasta yet.

3. Turn the stove to high and do other chores. The cozy will reduce the boiling time and save stove fuel.

Figure 7-2

Cozy cooking.

Velcro secures cozy skirt.

Cozy ½ inch below edge of pot.

Cozy band deflects cold wind and keeps heat in when cover is removed.

Exposed metal prevents cozy from burning.

Grab loop

Cover skirt

Cozy bands

Velcro

Mating Velcro

When done cooking, set hot pot on closed-cell foam pad.

4. When the water boils, turn down the heat to simmer and add the cereal, rice, pasta, or sauce mix. Stir vigorously till fixin's are blended and the water is boiling again. Then turn off the stove and set the pot on a square of closed-cell foam. Put on the cover and "top hat" and work the belly band down till it covers all the bare metal of the pot. Your food will slow cook in 20 minutes and stay hot for an hour.

5. Add contents of pasta packet to the simmering mixture and increase heat to boiling. Stir frequently until pasta is done—or use the cozy system explained earlier.

Tip: **If it's extremely cold and windy, place a second cozy (or a jacket) over the first when the meal is off the stove. I use a large, one-piece toaster cover for the second insulating layer. Be careful how you use commercial tea cozies and toaster covers: Most are made from acrylics that melt and shrink when exposed to heat.**

In 1982 I canoed the Hood River in the Northwest Territories with five friends. We relied on two Optimus 111B gasoline stoves for all our cooking and used an overturned canoe as a windscreen. Our stoves consumed six gallons of Coleman fuel in thirty-one days, or about a gallon and a half a week. We did not have pot cozies, so we were very careful to conserve fuel: For example, we boiled fresh-caught fish in soup instead of frying it, and we never baked or heated water for dishes.

I canoed the Hood again in 1992 with a crew of ten and brought double-insulated cozies for all my pots. I even made a special cozy with a "spout hole" for the twenty-four-cup teapot. Same two stoves as before, but four more people. We fried fish, boiled dish water, and routinely made popcorn. We used barely a gallon of fuel a week. Naturally, every meal I prepared was perfect!

Why Some Meals Fail

1 You haven't cooked the meat long enough. Dried meats require time to rehydrate, which is the reason why you should start them in cold water.

2. You burned the pasta—easy to do on a stove or campfire if you add everything at once. Pasta should always be added last—or for a class act, cooked separately.

3. Not enough water. I always increase suggested amounts by about 20 percent.

4. Insufficient spices. Use generous amounts of your all-spice and supplement with fresh or dried onions, celery, and green peppers.

5. Spoilage: Aluminum foil is a complete oxygen barrier. Foods packed in vacuum-sealed aluminum theoretically have an unlimited shelf life (same as canning). Plastic-bagged foods, on the other hand, merely "inhibit" the passage of oxygen molecules. In time (shelf life is about a year) aerobic bacteria in the food will cause spoilage. So unless you plan to freeze them, don't buy foods in September for use the following July. Your autumn bargain may become summer indigestion.

Add Fresh Vegetables to Your One-Pot Meals!

Fresh onions keep for weeks in the heat of summer, as long as they aren't bruised. Keep onions in a cotton bag; stow the bag inside a rigid container.

Tomatoes and green peppers will last about two weeks, if you follow these suggestions.

1. Wash the vegetables, then float them in a sink-full of drinking water that has been treated with about one-eighth cup (the amount isn't critical) of chlorine bleach. Allow the vegetables to soak for several minutes in the treated water before you dry and pack them away. The bleach will kill the surface bacteria that promotes spoilage. A similar procedure is used in some of America's finest restaurants to keep vegetables fresh.

You may use only a small piece of tomato or pepper at each meal. Cut off only the portion you need, and wash it in fresh water. Do not wash the entire vegetable! Doing so will introduce water-borne bacteria which may precipitate spoilage.

2. Separately wrap each vegetable in clean paper toweling. Pack towel-wrapped veggies in a paper or cotton sack and set the sack inside a teakettle or other crush-proof container. Do not seal vegetables in non-porous plastic! Semi-porous Ziploc vegetable bags are the notable exception.

Tip: **Red cabbage makes a tasty salad and keeps for weeks without refrigeration. Get ready for raves when, a week into your canoe or backpacking trip, you serve shredded red cabbage mixed with carrot and onion slices, topped with green olives and a favorite dressing. Really, now, when did you last have fresh greens on a wilderness adventure?**

Making Popcorn

If you're tired of trying to season popcorn in a pot that's too small, carry a large paper grocery sack on your next campout. Pour each batch of completed popcorn into the bag (don't use a plastic bag—hot corn will melt through it!) and season it there. Afterwards, burn the bag.

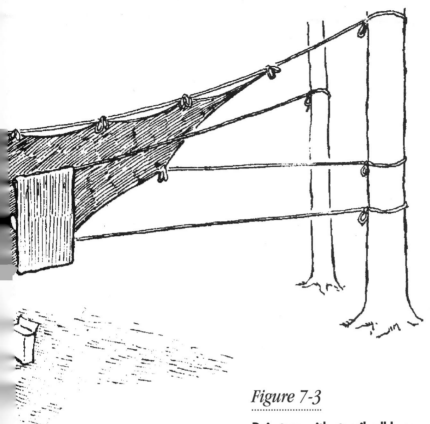

Figure 7-3

Rain tarp with utensil roll hung on the tight line below.

Cooking in the Rain

When rain threatens to spoil your stew, erect a 12-foot x 12-foot rain tarp and move the kitchen under it. Rig a tight line just beneath the fly and snap your utensil roll to the overhead cord (Figure 7-3). Now, everything from spices to spoons will be immediately available and protected from weather and the wet ground. (See my books *Camping's Top Secrets* or *Basic Essentials: Camping* for the specifics of fly rigging and the knots and hitches needed to rig a snug camp.)

In summary, an ounce of re-packing at home is worth a pound of fumbling afield. Plan, pre-measure, and test new food ideas—and food containers—in the comfort of your kitchen, not in a remote bush camp where the price of failure is high. And don't rely on culinary skill to outfox the environment. Only a well-rigged rainfly will do that!

On into Winter

I t's mid-February and ten above in northern Minnesota—a glorious day for traveling.

"Looks like a blue wax day," calls Willie. "Yeah," I mutter, and chalk one ski, fumble and drop the tube of wax into four foot snow drift. I dig hard with my poles and, with grit determination, herringbone up the tortuous trail. Thirty minutes later I reach the top, flushed and sweating, my senses not yet attuned to the crisp solitude of the lake country's winter white. I dream of camp, a roaring fire ... and Roger's chili.

I snap on my headlamp and peer at my watch: 5:00 P.M. and almost dark. The thermometer stands at twenty below.

The water in the big Sigg pot is near boiling, so I set the gallon milk carton of frozen chili into it. Soon the cardboard separates from its contents, and I remove it from the pot.

"Hey Marc, I need more water!"

"Poly bottles by the pulk," comes the reply. I pull one bottle from the snow and pour its contents into the steaming pot.

Twenty minutes later the chili boils, and as is the cook's prerogative, I try a spoon. Awful! It tastes like burnt peppermint.

"Hey, you guys," calls Marc. "Anybody seen the peppermint Schnapps?"

As you can see, subzero temperatures, poor light, and downright carelessness tend to complicate food preparation. Here are some ways to avoid the pitfalls of cooking in winter.

The Right Foods

You burn a lot more calories in winter than in summer. So load up on carbohydrates and increase fat intake to 35 or 40 percent of your total calories. Fatty sausages like salami, Cervalot, and pepperoni are ideal winter fare, but peanut butter (a summer favorite) is not. Try chiseling Peter Pan out of a poly bottle at fifteen below and you'll see why!

Cheese, another nutritious high-fat food, tastes like candle tallow when frozen. The solution is to thaw it in a parka pocket or melt it into the evening's spaghetti.

Food Preparation Tips

Low temperatures and an icy wind make even an efficient stove seem lazy. So burrow your kitchen deep into the snow, away from drafts. And bring much more stove fuel than you would in summer. A liter a day for a party of four is about right. Since a hot stove will melt

its way down through a snowbank, be sure to provide a stable support. An inverted pie tin, plywood square, or piece of closed-cell foam works well. Don't set stoves on snowshoes or fiberglass pulk's (sleds): the heat may warp them. It bears repeating that insulated pot cozies are a *must* in cold weather.

Cookware

Select your plastic cups and bowls carefully. Plastics that are brittle in the store may shatter afield. Give your plastic cookware the "home freezer test" before you commit to them in frigid temperatures.

Dishwashing

Bacteria are dormant in subfreezing temperatures, so you need not wash dishes at all—that is, as long as you don't share eating utensils with your friends! A lot of winter campers simply wipe out their bowls with snow and go about their business.

Frankly, I prefer a more civilized approach. I swirl and rinse (no soap!) cookware in boiling water, then call it quits. To keep my hands toasty warm and dry, I wear light wool gloves inside plastic-coated cotton ones.

Footloose

Standing around at twenty below waiting for a pot to boil can be a chilling experience, even with good boots on. A square of half-inch thick closed-cell foam will take the edge off what's underfoot and double as a sitting pad in camp.

A Beam into the Night

Meal preparation is necessarily complicated by the long winter nights which, in northern latitudes, may keep things blacked out for twelve hours or more. If you plan a predawn start or late-day finish, you'll need some sort of artificial light for cooking. Standard flashlights are inefficient in the cold, and candle lanterns don't put out enough light. Best to bring a miner's headlamp—the kind that takes four D cells. I use alkaline batteries and keep the battery pack warm inside my parka.

Frozen Liquids?

Freezing begins at the air interface of a liquid, so store your water bottles *upside down* in the snow. This way you can forgo the difficulty (impossibility) of removing frozen bottle caps.

Cooking Dangers

1. Be extremely careful around stoves when you're bundled up! Sub-zero clothing is a marvelous insulator. You may be fully afire and not know it until it's too late!

2. Always wear gloves when handling liquid stove fuels in sub-freezing weather. Liquid fuels freeze at much lower temperatures than water. Spill gas on your skin at 20 below and you'll suffer immediate frostbite!

Leftover Food

In summer you bury or pack out what you don't eat. In winter there is no biological decomposition, so you *must* pack out leftovers!

These are the basic cold-weather cooking tricks. To this, add a love of wintery white, a generous measure of camaraderie, and a mixture of care and competence, and you'll enjoy the worst of times on the best of terms.

Ethical
Concerns

Autumn mist in the backcountry. One last outing before the icy throes of winter—a final opportunity to camp and fish and to enjoy the good times that go with warm friendships, bountiful wilderness, and fire-brewed coffee served steaming hot on a frosty morning.

In the distance, snuggled in dense hardwoods, is the campsite that you discovered more than a decade ago. Hauntingly beautiful, it is your special place.

Excitedly, you shoulder your pack and struggle through lush vegetation to the clearing above. The view from the top is spectacular, just like you remembered it.

Then you see it: the remains of thoughtless campers who preceded you—broken beer bottles, rusty cans, scraps of Styrofoam, and fly-infested fish remains. Suddenly, this place is no longer special. It is a trash heap, an insult to man and God. A gnawing pain grows upward from the pit of your stomach and surfaces as rage. The spell is broken!

Ultimately, your anger subsides and you put your thoughts in order. The slobs who preceded you occupied this spot for the same reasons as you—beauty and solitude. But, unlike you, they had no feeling for the land and no knowledge of the proper way to treat it. Most likely, their actions were the result of ignorance rather than wanton disrespect.

Renewed interest in outdoor recreation has placed heavy demands on our wilderness areas. But simply sharing the backcountry with others will not ensure its survival. What will is an understanding of ecological relationships and a commitment to ethical land use procedures. Please pass on these tenets—with commitment and vehemence—to all who will listen!

Disposal of Human Waste and Food Remains

Bury these under a 4-inch soil cover *out of the main camping area*, and at least 100 feet from water. Shallow burial ensures rapid decomposition. If you have a lot of biodegradable waste, dig several cat holes to reduce the volume of waste in a given spot.

Do not scatter foodstuffs on the surface of the ground with the thought that animals will eat it. They surely will! And they'll bring their friends, again and again, often becoming vicious if they haven't gotten their fill.

Some campers cache their food in a tree to keep it out of reach of determined black bears. This is a good idea providing you don't use the same tree as everyone else! Bears are creatures of habit; once fed at a certain spot, they'll be back for more. And they're very adept at getting food packs down from trees. If they can't smell your food, they won't get it. Just seal your food in plastic so there are no odors, then set it in the woods (or tree it, if you prefer), well out of the immediate campsite.

Remember, too, that through classical conditioning, animals learn to associate certain containers with the presence of food. How else can you explain why bears bite open clothes packs and tin cans (no odor here)? For this reason, you should keep traditional food containers out-of-sight.

Fish remains should not be thrown into a lake or river under the guise that "fish or turtles will get 'em." Viscera breed bacteria (a health concern) that use up the oxygen for fish and aquatic life—the reason why you should always bury these products.

Note: **Never throw biodegradables into outhouses or Forest Service box latrines. Bears will knock box latrines off their foundations to get at the food inside!**

Cooking in the Outdoors

Cans, Foil, and Other Non-Biodegradables

You brought 'em in, you pack 'em out. Standard procedure is to burn out tin cans, flatten them with a rock, then carry them home. In areas where fires are not permitted, cans may be burned out on your trail stove—a one-minute process.

Where to Get Safe Water

Authorities advise you to boil, filter, or chemically treat all water taken from a questionable source—sound advice if you have the chemicals or equipment and the self-discipline to use them. I confess to laziness in this respect: invariably, I drink untreated water but I'm very careful where I take it. Here are the guidelines I follow:

1. Go well away from shore to get your drinking water. On a river, take your water upstream of the campsite.

2. Decay organisms generally prefer the shallows, so the deeper your water source, the better.

3. Avoid water that has a greenish color. This indicates the presence of algae and accompanying microorganisms. And stay away from backwaters, stagnant areas, and beaver dams and lodges. Beavers are the favored host of the *Giardia* parasite.

Water Treatment Procedures

Most pathogens are killed instantly when water reaches boiling. When boiling is impractical, use a chemical tablet (available at most pharmacies) or one of the ingenious filtration units sold at camping shops. Potable Aqua, Globaline, or other iodine-based chemicals are more reliable in cold or cloudy water than Halazone, which releases chlorine. If you select a commercial filter, make sure the filter pore size is small enough to remove *Giardia*.

You can also use liquid chlorine bleach with 4 to 6 percent available chlorine to purify water. Use two drops of bleach per quart of clear water and four drops per quart of cold or cloudy water. Let the treated water stand thirty minutes before drinking, longer if it is cold or cloudy.

Other Concerns

Bathing and washing: Swimming's fine, bathing is not, even if you use biodegradable soap. Remember, biodegradable products break down from bacterial action, which lowers dissolved oxygen levels in the waterway. Please soap up on land and rinse via a bucket brigade. Then … go swimming!

Cutting vegetation: It's unethical (and usually illegal) to cut green trees or branches. If you need a stick for roasting hot dogs, use a dead one.

Rain-proofing your tent: Please don't trench around your tent to provide guttering for surface water. Once erosion begins, it continues. Use a plastic groundcloth *inside* your tent to trap flowing ground water that gets in through floor seams.

Finally, please be sure your fire is *dead out* (feel it with your hand.) before you move on. If it's hot enough to burn your hand, it's hot enough to burn a forest!

Appendix 1
Trail Stove Maintenance Tips

1. For greatest efficiency and trouble-free operation, use Coleman or Balzo fuel (it's naptha, not white gas) in your gasoline stove. These pre-filtered fuels burn clean and have extremely high heat output.

2. Don't fill gasoline stoves more than three-fourths full. You need air space to generate pressure.

3. Empty the fuel from your stove after each trip, and burn dry what you can't pour out. Fuel left in stoves leaves varnishes that clog jets and filters—the major reason for stove failure.

4. Once a year (if you use your stove a lot) add a capful—no more— of Gumout Carburetor Cleaner to your stove along with a half tank of gas. Burn the stove dry. The Gumout will dissolve built-up varnishes.

5. Keep your stove in a fabric sack when it's not in use. This will prevent dust and debris from getting into the working parts.

6. Lubricate leather pump washers with high-temperature gun oil. Avoid use of multi-purpose and vegetable oils, which may break down and gum up valves.

7. If you store stove fuel over the winter, keep fuel containers nearly full to reduce oxidation. Oxygen promotes the formation of varnish, which clogs stoves (and gasoline engines).

Appendix 2

Common Weights and Useful Measurements

3 teaspoons = 1 tablespoon

2 tablespoons = 1 liquid ounce

16 tablespoons = 1 cup

1 cup = 8 ounces

2 cups = 1 pint

4 cups = 1 quart

½ lb. margarine = 1 cup

1 lb. of granulated sugar = 2 cups

1 lb. of brown sugar = 3 cups

1 cup chopped nuts = about ¼ lb.

64 marshmallows = 1 lb.

No. 10 can holds about 12 cups of water.

1 level full Sierra cup holds 1⅛ cups water.

1 standard-size plastic insulated cup holds 1⅓ cups water.

1 medium onion = 2 tablespoons of minced dry onions.

1 tablespoon of fresh herbs = ½ teaspoon of dried herbs or ¼ teaspoon of dried, powdered herbs.

1 cup sour milk = 1 cup milk into which 1 tablespoon vinegar has been stirred.

1 cup sour cream can be made by adding ⅓ cup butter, ⅔ cup milk and 1 tablespoon vinegar.

Index